Predators of the Sea

Text by Mary Jo Rhodes and David Hall
Photographs by David Hall

Undersea Encounters

Children's Press®
A Division of Scholastic Inc.
New York   Toronto   London   Auckland   Sydney
Mexico City   New Delhi   Hong Kong
Danbury, Connecticut

Library of Congress Cataloging-in-Publication Data

Rhodes, Mary Jo, 1957-
    Predators of the sea / text by Mary Jo Rhodes and David Hall; photographs by David Hall.
        p. cm. (Undersea encounters)
    Includes bibliographical references.
    ISBN-10: 0-516-24399-3 (lib. bdg.)   0-516-25465-0 (pbk.)
    ISBN-13: 978-0-516-24399-3 (lib. bdg.)   978-0-516-25465-4 (pbk.)
    1. Predatory marine animals—Juvenile literature. I. Hall, David, 1943 Oct. 2– II. Title.
III. Series.
    QL122.2.R492 2006
    591.5'3'09162—dc22

                                    2005024566

*To my wife and diving partner, Gayle Jamison, whose support and encouragement
have made this book series possible.
—D. H.
To my son Tim, who taught me to appreciate sharks and from whom I've learned
so much about these amazing animals.
—M. J. R.*

All photographs © 2007 by David Hall except: Brandon Cole Marine Photography: 15
inset top (Brandon Cole); Nature Picture Library Ltd./Alan James: 15 inset bottom.

The snakelike moray eel can squeeze into tight spaces.
pg. **35**

The mako shark's streamlined body is built for speed.
pg. **6**

Predators of the Sea

Steer clear of the blue-ringed octopus— its bite is deadly!
pg. **26**

Barracudas are predators
that rely upon speed to
catch their prey.

chapter 1

Speedy Undersea Predators

From tiny snails to great whales, most animals in the sea are **predators**. A predator is an animal that hunts and eats other animals. You might think that all predators are big animals with sharp teeth, such as sharks. But most predators aren't very large, and many don't even have teeth.

Before a predator can eat, it must first catch its **prey**. In the open ocean, small fish and other prey rely on speed to avoid being caught. A successful predator must be faster than its prey in this deadly game of tag. Swift predators have smooth, streamlined bodies that allow them to move quickly through the water. Speedy undersea predators include squids, fish, sea mammals, and seabirds.

Fish Predators

The mako shark is a close relative of the great white shark. It is not as large as a great white, but it can swim much faster. Makos are the fastest of

Mako sharks can grow to be about 13 feet (4 meters) long and weigh up to 1,000 pounds (450 kilograms).

all sharks. They are quick and powerful enough to hunt large, swift prey such as tuna and swordfish.

Unlike the mako shark which hunts in the open sea, barracudas live on reefs closer to land. Smaller kinds, or **species**, of barracuda swim in schools. But the largest species, the 5-foot (1.5 m) great barracuda, usually hunts alone. All barracudas are built for short bursts of speed and have powerful jaws for grabbing their prey.

The great barracuda relies on speed and surprise to catch smaller fish.

Mako Shark Fact

Mako sharks can swim more than 40 miles (64 kilometers) per hour—much faster than most motorboats.

Penguins are excellent divers and fast swimmers that hunt small fish.

Dolphins locate prey underwater by making sounds and listening for the echoes.

Other Speedy Predators

Seabirds such as gulls and pelicans are also ocean predators. Of all the seabirds, penguins are the best adapted to ocean life. They cannot fly in the air, but they use their wings to "fly" through the water. Penguins are speedy swimmers that catch and eat many kinds of fish.

Sea mammals are also quick-moving ocean predators. Dolphins, seals, and sea lions use their speed and athletic abilities to catch fish. When looking for food, dolphins make clicking noises and listen for the echoes. This helps them locate fish in murky water. They sometimes use an especially loud noise to stun a fish that is hiding under the sand.

Squids are the fastest ocean-dwelling **invertebrates**, or animals without backbones. They use their speed to catch fish. When a squid gets close to a fish, it shoots out two extra-long arms, called tentacles, to grab its prey.

Squids are the fastest invertebrate predators. They use their long tentacles to grab small fish.

A butterflyfish has a long, slender snout that is perfect for reaching into hard coral skeletons and grazing on coral **polyps**.

chapter 2

Grazing in the Sea

On land, animals such as rabbits and deer graze, or feed, on grass and other plants. Some undersea predators also graze, but not on plants. They nibble on corals, sponges, and other animals attached to the sea bottom. These attached animals may seem like plants because they don't move very much.

Grazing Snails

Wentletraps (WEN-til-traps) are snails that graze on cup corals. These yellow

A pair of wentletrap snails feeds on orange tube corals.

or orange snails get their color from the corals they eat. This helps to disguise them and keeps them safe from other predators.

Nudibranchs (NEW-duh-branks) are sea slugs, or snails without shells. They graze on many bottom-dwelling animals, such as sea anemones (uh-NEM-uh-neez), sponges, and sea squirts.

A nudibranch munches on blue-and-yellow sea squirts.

A small filefish grazes on the polyps of a pink soft coral colony.

Grazing Fish

Fish predators also graze on corals, sponges, and other invertebrate animals. Coral-eating fish have long snouts and small mouths. This helps them reach the polyps that live in small nooks within the coral structure. These coral predators include filefish and butterflyfish. Angelfish are predators that often graze on sponges.

Open Wide!

Some of the largest animals in the sea prey on some of the smallest ones. These large predators often swim with their mouths wide open. The seawater that enters is strained to remove prey such as small fish or **crustaceans**.

A 15-foot (4.6 m) manta ray swims with its mouth wide open as it feeds on a swarm of tiny crustaceans.

A humpback whale has folds, or pleats, in its throat. They allow the whale's throat to expand so that it can take a huge gulp of water containing hundreds of small fish.

The 33-foot (10-m) basking shark is the world's second largest fish. It swims with a wide-open mouth, capturing small fish and other tiny animals.

The mantis shrimp is a small but powerful crustacean predator. It uses its front claws like hammers to smash the shell of its prey.

chapter 3

Breaking and Entering

Hard shells protect the soft bodies of snails, scallops, and many other sea animals. Some predators are strong enough to crush these shells. A few predators can force open the shells of clams or scallops. Other predators are able to drill a hole through the shell to get at the tasty animal inside.

Jaws That Crush

A few large predators have jaws strong enough to crush the thickest shell.

The leopard shark has powerful jaws for breaking open the shells of large mollusks.

These predators include logger-head sea turtles, leopard sharks, and eagle rays. Leopard sharks live on the ocean floor where they hunt for snails, clams, and scallops. These 10-foot (3-m) sharks have strong jaws and can easily crush the shells of large **mollusks**.

Powerful Claws

Some invertebrate predators have powerful claws for cracking or crushing the shells of their prey. These animals are known as crustaceans and include crabs, lobsters, and shrimps.

Mantis Shrimp Fact

Mantis shrimps cannot be kept in an ordinary aquarium. Their hammerlike claws can smash right through the glass!

18

Mantis shrimps have claws that work like hammers to smash the shells of their prey. The northern lobster has two different kinds of claws. It has a sharp claw for cutting and a thick claw for crushing shells.

A northern lobster snacks on an arm that it has torn off of a sea star.

A Deadly Hug

Sea stars, often called starfish, are invertebrate predators with five or more arms. A hungry sea star wraps its arms around a clam or mussel. It grips both halves of the shell with hundreds of small tube feet like tiny suction cups. The sea star steadily pulls the shell apart, waiting for the clam to tire. When the shell begins to open, the sea star

Tiny tube feet on the underside of a sea star grip the shell of a clam. The star will slowly pull the shell open to get at the clam inside.

pushes its stomach through the opening and digests the clam.

A Sharp Tongue

Like clams and oysters, sea snails are mollusks. This, however, doesn't stop some of them from preying on their relatives. A snail predator uses its sharp tongue, or **radula**, to drill a hole through the shells of its prey. Moon snails drill holes in clam and oyster shells. Bonnet shell snails prey on small sea urchins, which are spiny, shelled animals related to sea stars.

A bonnet shell snail (left) attacks a spiny heart urchin. The urchin is trying to escape by tunneling into the sand.

Attacking Sharp Spines

Sea urchins have long, sharp spines for protection. But these spines won't stop a hungry titan triggerfish. The triggerfish uses its strong teeth and jaws to break off the urchin's spines two or three at a time.

Jellyfish have tentacles lined with stingers used for capturing and killing small fish and other prey.

chapter 4

Predators with Poison

How does a slow-moving predator catch faster prey? How can a small animal overcome a larger one? The answer is **venom**. Venom is poison delivered by a bite or sting. A predator with venom uses its poison to disable a larger or faster animal.

Jellyfish

Jellyfish and their relatives are **cnidarians**. This invertebrate group also includes corals and sea anemones.

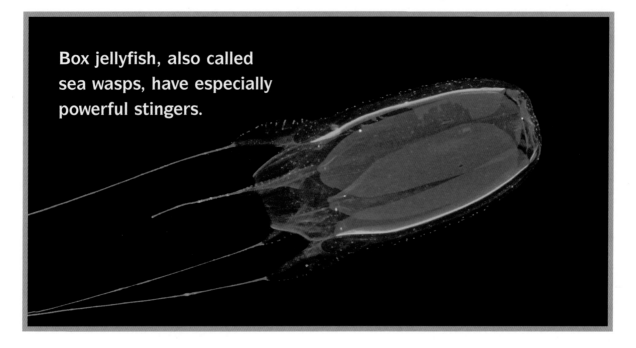

Box jellyfish, also called sea wasps, have especially powerful stingers.

All of these animals have tentacles covered with poison stingers.

A jellyfish swims by opening and closing its bell-shaped body like an umbrella. Most jellyfish have a round body, but box jellyfish have a square shape. Box jellyfish venom is especially powerful and quickly kills fish and other prey. One kind of box jellyfish in Australia has the most deadly venom of any sea animal. A sting from this jellyfish can kill a person in less than five minutes.

Venomous Mollusks

Two different kinds of mollusks use poison to overcome their prey. Cones are poisonous snails. They use their radula like a harpoon to inject venom into their prey. Many cones prey on other mollusks and on worms, but some prey on fish. The fish-eating geographic cone has venom so powerful that it can kill a person.

The head end of this cone snail is on the right. The snail's siphon tube (mouth) is pointing up and its venomous radula is pointing down and to the right.

The tiny blue-ringed octopus uses its powerful poison to kill crabs and other prey. The bright-blue rings warn other animals to leave this dangerous octopus alone.

Although they look very different from snails, octopuses are also mollusks. Octopuses have venom that enters the wound when they bite. The blue-ringed octopus is the most venomous octopus of all. This tiny predator is about the size of a golf ball and can overcome a crab larger than

Blue-ringed Octopus Fact

A person bitten by a blue-ringed octopus may die when the muscles needed for breathing become paralyzed.

itself. Sometimes it does this by releasing venom into the water near the crab. The poison is probably taken into the crab's body through its **gills**.

Venomous Snakes

Sea snakes are related to cobras. Most have a venomous bite, and their venom is very deadly. Sea snakes hunt for moray eels and other fish in the holes and cracks of coral reefs. After a single bite, the venom kills a fish quickly. The snake can then swallow its meal without a struggle.

There are about fifty species of venomous sea snakes. They can be found in the tropical Pacific and Indian oceans.

Can you see the scorpionfish in this photograph? Scorpionfish are experts at blending in with their surroundings.

chapter 5

Hidden Predators

Imagine for a moment that there are invisible monsters hiding in your neighborhood. Imagine that they appear suddenly and swallow people whole. Wouldn't you be afraid to go outside?

In the ocean, small fish have to deal with this problem. There are hungry, invisible predators everywhere. These predators blend in with their surroundings so effectively that they do not need to chase their prey. They lie in wait for their prey to come to them.

Color-Changing Experts

Scorpionfish are color-changing experts. They **camouflage** themselves cleverly by changing color to match their surroundings. There are many different kinds of scorpionfish, and all of them are predators. They are named for their venomous fin spines, which help protect them from larger predators.

This leaf scorpionfish has captured a small fish known as a basslet. Scorpionfish are hidden predators that ambush their prey.

Stonefish are especially well-disguised members of the scorpionfish family. This one looks like a rock covered with seaweed.

The body of the leaf scorpionfish is so flat that it resembles a dead leaf. The bearded scorpionfish has skin growths that disguise its outline. The 12-inch (30-centimeter) stonefish has a large head and a small tail. It cannot swim well, but that doesn't matter—a well-disguised predator doesn't need to be a good swimmer.

31

A camouflaged flounder swallows a long, thin pipefish. The pipefish was disguised as a stick, but the flounder wasn't fooled.

Hidden in the Sand

There are many predators hidden on sandy sea bottoms. Flounders are fish predators with flat bodies. They can change color instantly to blend in with different kinds of sand. The lizardfish also changes color to match sand. Its needle-sharp teeth are curved inward. Once caught, a small fish can only

Flounder Fact

Both eyes of an adult flounder are located on the same side of its head. Young baby flounders look like other fish. As they grow, one eye gradually moves to the other side!

This lizardfish has captured a fangblenny. The blenny is struggling to free itself, but the lizardfish's sharp teeth make it difficult to escape.

move in one direction—down the throat of the lizardfish.

The stargazer is a hidden predator that buries itself in sand. Its eyes are located on the top of its head, so it appears to be gazing at the sky. Some stargazers wiggle a small lure inside their mouths, to attract prey closer, to within striking distance.

Stargazers bury themselves in sand, often with only their eyes showing.

The Bobbit worm is a giant predator that lives in a sand burrow. This monster has huge jaws much wider than its own body. The largest Bobbit worms may grow to be 10 feet (3 m) long. They feed by grabbing passing fish and dragging them down into their burrows.

A giant Bobbit worm waits at the opening of its burrow for a fish to pass overhead. This 10-foot (3-m) monster with powerful jaws hunts only at night.

Under Cover of Darkness

Moray eels are predatory fish with snakelike bodies and long, sharp teeth. Their shape allows them to fit into tight spaces when searching for prey. Morays hunt mostly at night for prey that includes fish, octopuses, and crustaceans.

▼ Blue ribbon eel

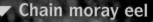

▼ Chain moray eel

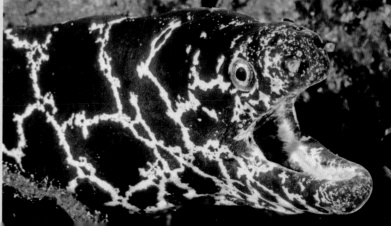

The weedy scorpionfish is
a predator that looks like
a feather star, a plantlike
sea star relative.

chapter 6

Predators in Disguise

A predator that takes on the appearance of another animal is a **mimic**. Mimic predators fool their prey by looking like harmless animals such as feather stars, corals, or sponges.

In addition to disguising their appearance, some mimics use bait. Just like a person fishing, a frogfish attracts its prey by wiggling a worm-like lure.

When a weedy scorpionfish opens its huge mouth quickly, a nearby small fish will be sucked in.

Feather Star Mimic

The weedy scorpionfish mimics plantlike sea star relatives called feather stars. Small fish shelter among the long, feathery arms of these harmless animals. But any fish that mistakes a scorpion-fish for a feather star will soon become a meal.

Coral Mimic

The predatory trumpetfish uses a number of sneaky tactics to disguise its presence. Sometimes it hides behind a harmless plant-eater such as a parrotfish. At other times the trumpetfish uses a head-down position to mimic coral branches. Ever so slowly, it inches toward a small fish. At the last second, the trumpetfish darts forward and grabs its prey.

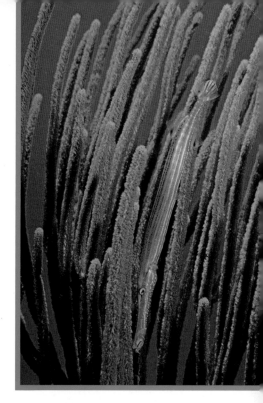

Floating head down, a slender trumpetfish mimics the appearance of the coral branches around it.

Cleaner Fish Mimic

Cleaners are small fish that remove harmful **parasites** and dead skin from other fish. The fangblenny closely mimics the appearance of a common cleaner fish. Expecting to be cleaned, other fish allow the mimic to approach. But when the fangblenny gets close, it doesn't clean—it bites!

The fangblenny is a predator that mimics the appearance of harmless cleaner fish.

Fishing with Bait

Frogfish, or anglerfish, use a lure to attract their prey.
The frogfish wiggles the lure to make it seem alive.
Frogfish have huge mouths and big stomachs. They
can swallow prey that is larger than they are!

Frogfish are very well disguised.
They are able to change color
and often look like nearby
sponges.

The tassled anglerfish
resembles a seaweed-
covered rock. It uses a
wormlike lure to attract
small fish.

An orange longlure frogfish mimics the appearance of nearby sponges.

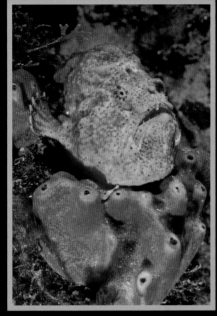

A yellow frogfish waves its lure above its head to attract prey.

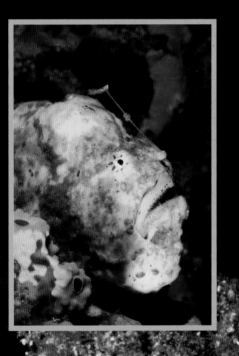

41

Epilogue:
The Most Dangerous Predator

The most dangerous predator of the sea is not a shark. To see it, you don't have to visit an aquarium or go scuba diving—just look in a mirror! Humans are the oceans' top predators.

People go to sea in **factory ships** armed with modern "weapons." They use mile-long drift nets and longlines with hundreds of baited hooks. Humans have become very good at catching fish. Once-common food fish—such as cod, swordfish, and tuna—are now much harder to find.

Some fishing methods cause the accidental deaths of many sea turtles, dolphins, and seabirds. Other fishing methods are simply cruel and wasteful. Some people catch sharks and cut off their fins. The animals are then thrown back

This female silvertip shark avoided being caught but still has a fishhook in the corner of her mouth.

in the water to die. The fins are sold for a high price to chefs who use them to make shark fin soup, considered a special treat in some cultures.

We must learn that all life in the ocean requires a healthy balance between predators and prey. If we respect that balance, the oceans will continue to inspire us and provide us with food.

Glossary

camouflage (**KAM-uh-flahz**) the ability of an animal to blend in with its surroundings through color, shape, or other means *(pg. 30)*

cnidarians (**ni-DARE-ee-enz**) invertebrate animals with tentacles and stingers; sea anemones, corals, hydroids, and jellyfish are cnidarians *(pg. 23)*

crustaceans (**kruhss-TAY-shunz**) invertebrate animals with jointed legs and two pairs of antennae, or feelers; crabs, lobsters, and shrimps are examples of crustaceans *(pg. 14)*

factory ships (**FAK-tree SHIPS**) ships that have equipment onboard to process a fish catch while at sea *(pg. 42)*

gills (**GILZ**) organs used for getting oxygen from water *(pg. 27)*

invertebrates (**in-VUR-tuh-brits**) animals without backbones or inner skeletons *(pg. 9)*

mimic (**MIM-ik**) an animal that is disguised as something else *(pg. 37)*

mollusks (**MOL-uhsks**) soft-bodied invertebrate animals that are often protected by an outer shell *(pg. 18)*

parasites (**PA-ruh-sites**) animals that live on or inside of other animals and cause harm *(pg. 39)*

polyps (**POL-ips**) individual coral animals with tentacles surrounding a central mouth *(pg. 10)*

predators (**PRED-uh-turz**) animals that hunt and eat other animals for food *(pg. 5)*

prey (**PRAY**) an animal that is killed and eaten by another animal *(pg. 5)*

radula (**RAD-yu-luh**) the sharp tongue of a mollusk, used for feeding *(pg. 20)*

species (**SPEE-seez**) a particular kind of animal or plant *(pg. 7)*

venom (**VEN-uhm**) a poison that is injected by biting or stinging *(pg. 23)*

Learn More About Predators of the Sea

Books

Cole, Melissa and Brandon. *Sharks.* Woodbridge, Conn.: Blackbirch Press, 2001.

Rhodes, Mary Jo, and David Hall. *Life in a Kelp Forest.* Danbury, Conn.: Children's Press, 2005.

Rhodes, Mary Jo, and David Hall. *Survival Secrets of Sea Animals.* Danbury, Conn.: Children's Press, 2007.

Solway, Andrew. *Killer Fish.* Chicago: Heinemann, 2005.

Web Sites

Coral Reef Connections: Predator and Prey
http://www.pbs.org/wgbh/evolution/survival/coral/predators.html

Predators of the Reef
http://bird.miamisci.org/oceans/coralreef/predators/

Undersea Predators
www.seaphotos.com/predators.html

Index

About the Authors

With degrees in zoology and medicine, **David Hall** has worked for the past twenty-five years as both a wildlife photojournalist and a physician. His articles and photographs have appeared in hundreds of calendars, books, and magazines, including *National Geographic, Smithsonian, Natural History*, and *Ranger Rick*. His underwater images have won many major awards, including Nature's Best, BBC Wildlife Photographer of the Year, and Festival Mondial de l'Image Sous-Marine. To see more of David's work, visit www.seaphotos.com.

Mary Jo Rhodes received her master's degree in library service from Columbia University and was a librarian for the Brooklyn Public Library. She later worked for ten years in children's book publishing in New York City. Mary Jo lives with her husband, John Rounds, and teenage sons, Jeremy and Tim, in Hoboken, New Jersey. To learn more about Mary Jo Rhodes and her books, visit www.maryjorhodes.com.

About the Consultants

Karen Gowlett-Holmes is an expert on the classification of marine invertebrates. She has worked as Collection Manager of Marine Invertebrates for the South Australia Museum and for the Australian scientific research organization, CSIRO. Karen has published more than forty scientific papers.

Gene Helfman is an expert on the behavior and ecology of fishes. He is a professor of ecology at the University of Georgia where he teaches ichthyology and conservation biology. Gene is the author of more than fifty scientific papers and first author of the widely used textbook *The Diversity of Fishes*.